Pe

*Text:* Chiz Dakin

*Series editor:* Tony Bowerman

*Photographs:* Chiz Dakin, Dennis Kelsall, James Grant Photograpy, Paul Newcombe Photography, Shutterstock, Dreamstime, Alamy, Adobe Stock

*Design:* Carl Rogers and Laura Hodgkinson

Ordnance Survey Licensed Mapping

OS Partner

**Northern Eye Books**

**Northern Eye Books**

**ISBN 978-1-908632-78-4**

*A CIP catalogue record for this book is available from the British Library.*

**www.northerneyebooks.co.uk**

**Cover:** *Mam Tor ridge (Walk 10)*

*First published in 2018 by*

**Northern Eye Books Limited**
*Northern Eye Books, Tattenhall, Cheshire CH3 9PX*

tony@northerneyebooks.com

www.northerneyebooks.co.uk

@northerneyebooks

@northerneyeboo

*For sales enquiries, please call 01928 723 744*

# Contents

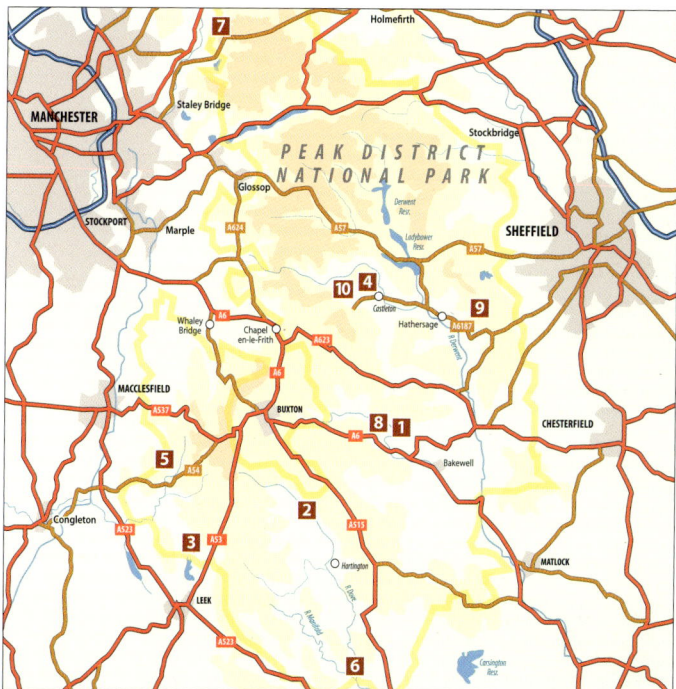

# England's First **National Park**

CREATED IN 1951, THE PEAK DISTRICT NATIONAL PARK extends over six counties and is the second most visited of Britain's National Parks. Its highest point lies upon the seemingly remote Kinder Plateau, where a mass trespass in 1932 marked the turning point in a long and sometimes bitter campaign that led to the creation of Britain's National Parks and the open access we enjoy today.

The high, peaty moorlands of the northern Dark Peak are founded on gritstone, their stark grandeur accentuated by impressive weatherworn tors and edges. The moors extend out of the Pennines in two horns that enclose the limestone plateau of the White Peak, an upland pasture cleft by narrow gorges and dales. The transition between the two is startlingly abrupt and each has a distinctive character and beauty all its own; the wild openness of the north contrasting with the south's intimate landscape dotted with small villages and criss-crossed by old lanes.

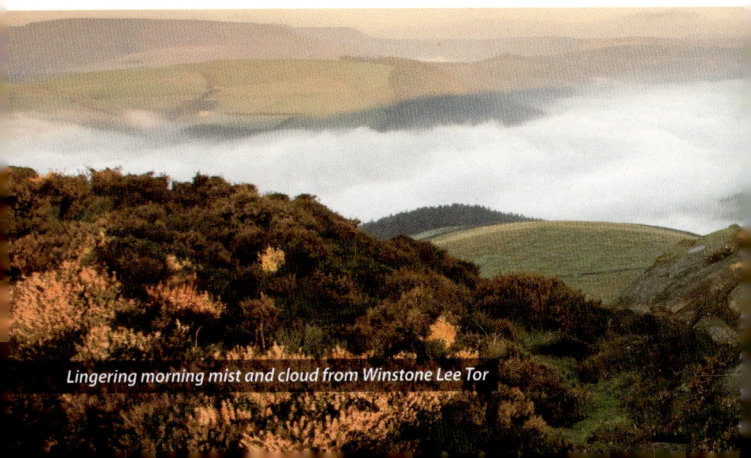

*Lingering morning mist and cloud from Winstone Lee Tor*

# The **Peak District's** Finest Views

Views are why many of us venture into the hills and countryside in the first place. Nothing beats a sweeping view from a moorland edge or hill, or an extensive panorama over a pleasant valley. Sometimes it's just the simple pleasure of the patterns of light and shade, the textures and colours of the woodland or the flowing beauty of the stream we're walking beside. But typically there's a feeling that you've earned a great view through sheer effort — even if the easiest approach had been taken to reach it. Perhaps that's why so many of the great Peak District views are atop minor summits, at moorland edges, or overlooking deep valleys.

*"And after many a tug and weary Strain,*

*Halfe breathless, they the Summit do gain."*

Thomas Hobbes, *De Mirabilis Pecci*, 1677

# TOP 10 **Walks:** Walks to Viewpoints

WHAT MAKES ONE VIEW more pleasing to the eye than another is always a matter of personal preference, but as a walker, typically some form of effort will have been required to attain it. And then the fabulous view becomes the just reward! There is variety though — from windswept gritstone edges to deep limestone ravines; hidden viewpoints once lost to walkers, to wide open moorland plateaus. These ten walks are selected for their variety of scenery, but all have commanding viewpoints over the surrounding terrain.

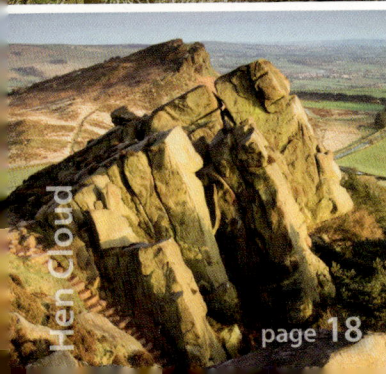

Monsal Head page 8

High Wheeldon page 12

Hen Cloud page 18

Lose Hill page 24

Shutlingsloe

Thorpe Cloud

Alderman's Hill

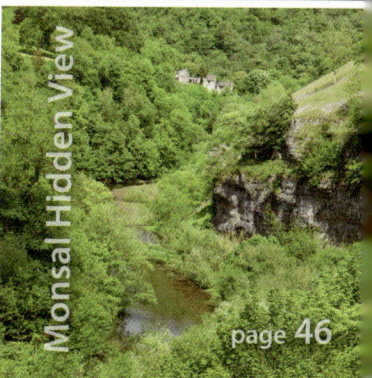

Monsal Hidden View

Burbage Valley Tors

Mam Tor

*The impressive Monsal Viaduct from the high valley sides to the south*

# Monsal Head

*Is this the White Peak's premier viewpoint? Stunning panoramic views of Monsal Dale and its iconic viaduct*

**What to expect:**
*Field paths, rail-trail and viaduct, steep woodland, riverside, and gentle re-ascent.*

**Distance/Time:** 5 kilometres/ 3 miles. Allow 1½ hours

**Start:** Large car park behind Monsal Head Hotel

**Grid Ref:** SK 185 715

**Ordnance Survey Map:** Explorer OL24 Peak District: White Peak area: *Buxton, Bakewell, Matlock & Dovedale*

**After the Walk:** Monsal Head Hotel, Monsal Head, Nr. Bakewell, Derbyshire DE45 1NL | 01629 640 250 | www.monsalhead.com

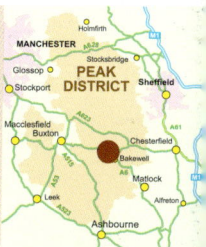

## Walk outline

*Starting high up by the Monsal Head Hotel, a short walk leads down a quiet lane to fields. These join the easy going Monsal Trail to enter the Headstone tunnel. Across the viaduct over Monsal Dale, the path descends to the riverbank and curves back under the viaduct. Pass a pleasant weir, go over a footbridge and it's a gentle climb back to the grandest view of them all — the panorama from Monsal Head.*

## Monsal Head

Perched high above a bend of the River Wye, Monsal Head is a stunning viewpoint and one of the Peak District's true visitor 'honeypots'. Limestone crags tower above woods and meadows that frame a ribbon of reflective river. Although the original railway line was once derided by John Ruskin as *'a method of exchanging fools between Buxton and Bakewell'*, the stone viaduct is now an integral part of the view. With the smoke and noise of the steam engines long gone, the valley has almost returned to Ruskin's *'rocky valley between Buxton and Bakewell … divine as the Vale of Tempe ...'*

Monsal Head ice-cream

Jacob's Ladder

## The Walk

**1.** Cross the road by the **Monsal Head Hotel** and take a lane to 'Little Longstone'. The pavement ends just past 'The Hollow' bed and breakfast.

**2.** Take the rightmost of two footpaths opposite, going through a gate and heading towards the 'Monsal Trail'. The path heads down a wide and shallow grassy vale broken into a couple of fields, with cattle often present. Beyond the second field gate, the path runs below an **embankment wall** (holding back the old railway trackbed), until a **stepped stile** gives access onto the **Monsal Trail**.

**3.** Turn right along the Trail and continue for a kilometre or so to the **Monsal Viaduct**, passing under a road bridge and through the **Headstone Tunnel**.

*As you approach the road overbridge, look on the left side of the cutting for a clear band of 'pancake layered' rock in the middle of the typical limestone. This is shale — the third, and lesser-known, type of rock in the Peak District — which is more common around Mam Tor.*

**4.** About 50 metres past the viaduct turn right onto a bridleway to 'Monsal Head via Netherdale'. This descends diagonally through woodland to a riverside path opposite **Uppermill**.

**5.** Turn right along the path and follow it around to the right, **under the viaduct** and through a **squeeze stile** into the broad, open meadow beside the river. As the meadow comes to an end, the path keeps going as a dirt track. Leave the open access land at a small gate and pass the impressive **weir**.

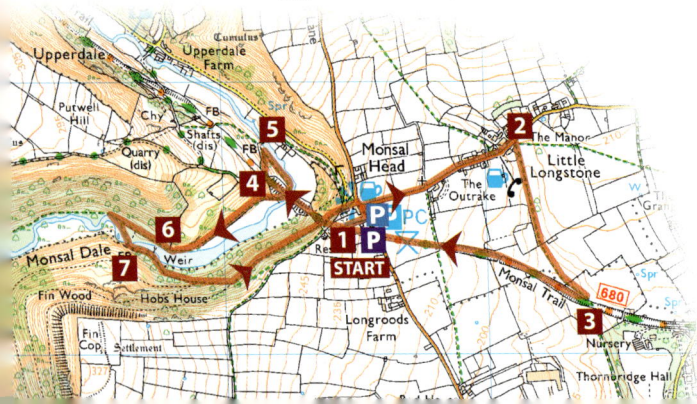

*High summer brings lush growth to the banks of the River Wye*

**6.** Keep a look out for the footbridge on the left which you will soon be taking, but for now, continue as far down the track as you feel like, before retracing your steps to cross the **footbridge** over the river.

**7.** The route now bends back along the other river bank, past the weir and through a gate. The path becomes increasingly narrow as it bends slightly away from the river before rising gently up the wooded hillside.

Leave the woodland at a gate and continue a short distance up to **Monsal Head**, with fabulous views now far below you.

Follow the road around the **Monsal Head Hotel** to return to the start and complete the walk. ♦

### Dukes and diversions

*The Monsal Trail runs along the line of the 1863 Midland Railway line between Derby and Manchester. Objections by the Dukes of Devonshire and Rutland to its progress through their Chatsworth and Haddon estates meant the route was diverted up the Wye Valley. Rutland eventually allowed a tunnel through Haddon, but Devonshire only relented when it was too late. Interestingly, both were given 'personal' stations: Bakewell for Rutland and Hassop for Devonshire.*

*Parkhouse and Chrome Hills seen from the edge of Crowdecote*

# High Wheeldon

*A fantastic viewpoint over the Upper Dove and Manifold Valleys that's surprisingly easy to reach via access land*

**What to expect:**
*Occasionally boggy, one steep descent (avoidable by road detour).*

**Distance/Time:** 6.5 kilometres/ 4 miles. Allow 2½ hours

**Start:** Market place or roadside parking in Longnor

**Grid Ref:** SK 088 649

**Ordnance Survey Map:** Explorer OL24 Peak District: White Peak area: *Buxton, Bakewell, Matlock & Dovedale*

**After the Walk:** Ye Olde Cheshire Cheese, High Street, Longnor, Buxton SK17 ONS | 01298 83218

## Walk Outline

*Head out through farmland on the gentle slopes of the Manifold Valley to a country lane. There's a steep descent into the Upper Dove Valley which can be challenging if wet (if so use the road), before tarmac eases the way up to access land. High pasture leads to the trig point view, then it's a steep grassy descent down to another short section of lane. A gentle path across meadowland in the valley bottom leads to a concrete track rising steadily back to the start.*

## High Wheeldon

With its fabulous views over the Upper Dove and Manifold valleys, spiky topped limestone outcrops of Hitter, Parkhouse and Chrome Hills and the high Derbyshire plateau, High Wheeldon would have been a commanding site for a castle. Yet its earliest known inhabitants were more likely to have lived underground in Fox Hole Cave (roughly 30 metres along the ridge from the summit). Sadly the chambers below are barred, but try to imagine people coming and going some 12,000 years ago, perhaps sheltering or bringing antler-tipped spears as grave goods to an ancient burial site.

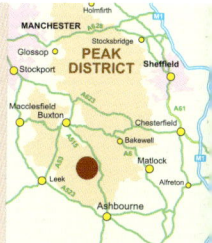

*Fox Hole Cave*

*Curlew*

## The Walk

**1.** Head out of **Longnor's market place** and walk past **Ye Olde Cheshire Cheese**. (In winter or wet conditions, to avoid a slippery descent into teh Dove Valley, continue along the road here and fork left at the junction, rejoining the main route at the **Pack Horse Inn**.)

Otherwise, take the second tarmac track on your right through a **farmyard**, signposted for 'Brundall'. After a couple of gates, cross a small field diagonally right to a stile. Follow the wall to the left, then as the wall turns away from the footpath, contour across a series of narrow sloping fields.

**2.** Close to **Crofts Farm**, bend sharp right to a metal gate, cross a small field diagonally left, then go through a gate in a fence below the **farm buildings**. Maintain your gently descending line across a larger field, soon gaining a hawthorn-lined wall on your left. As the hawthorns end, cross to the other side of the wall. The path funnels through a gate into the next field, then meets a vehicle track rising up the field.

**3.** Continue about 20 metres up the track and go through a **squeeze stile** on the left by the field edge. The path now follows the top of the field, passes a house then leads into a large sloping meadow. Head for the top right corner, and through another **squeeze stile** into a smaller field. Stay beside the

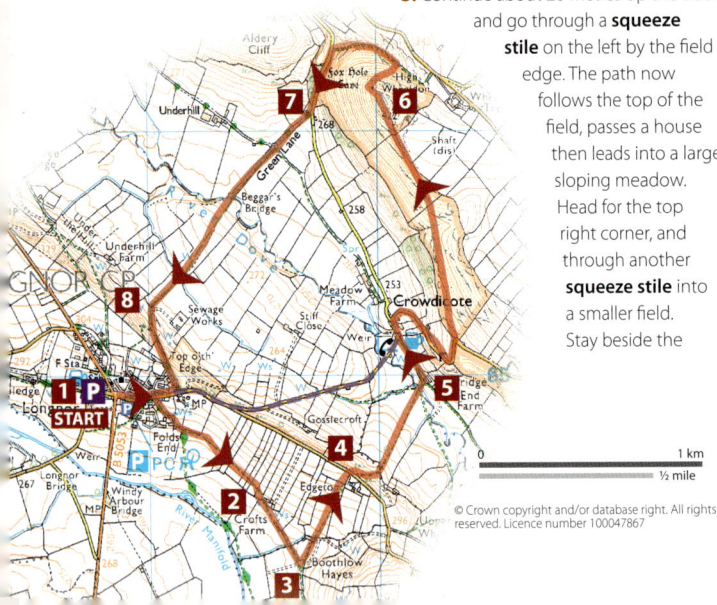

*The summit of High Wheeldon is a superb viewpoint*

righthand wall then turn right onto a country lane.

**4.** Take a footpath almost opposite and at the top of a steep scarp slope. Ensure you find the correct descent line here: a well-worn dirt path about 20 metres right of the stile (rather than the grassy dip through the hedge immediately opposite the stile). Drop steeply through woodland (if wet, it's best to take the road to Crowdecote) and cross a large field, where the gradient eases down to the **River Dove**.

**5.** Cross the **bridge** then follow a stony track leftwards below **Bridge End Farm** into **Crowdecote**. Turn right onto a quiet but narrow road passing the **Pack Horse Inn**, rising up a series of **hairpin bends** to a gate leftwards into access land. Follow white-topped waymarkers, rising gently across fields and a dry stream valley ahead. Maintain your direction across another long field, then rise more steeply to the **trig point**.

*Crowdecote was on a junction of trade routes before the 16th century inn was built and busy Longnor market gained*

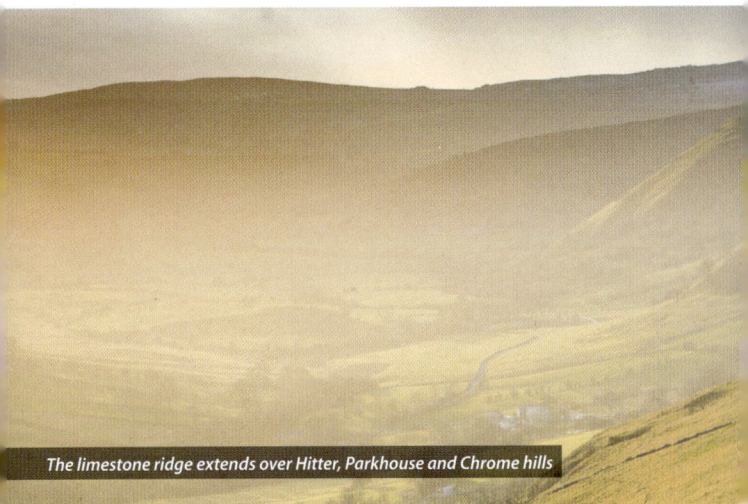

*The limestone ridge extends over Hitter, Parkhouse and Chrome hills*

*its charter. Probably originating as a packhorse route, the construction of the 18th century turnpike from Hassop to Leek and Newcastle must have boosted trade at the inn.*

**6.** Detour 30 metres along the ridge to visit **Fox Hole Cave**.

*Hidden on the side of the summit ridge, lies a gated passageway into an ancient limestone cave which has been inhabited by humans at varying times since the Stone Age. Rediscovered in 1928 during the rescue of a dog from an apparent fox hole, subsequent archaeological excavation has produced a treasure trove of extremely ancient finds including a bear skull and*

*fragments of cave lion bones. Cave lions became extinct about 13000 years ago.*

*The National Trust (Ilam and White Peak) runs an infrequent summer tour of the caves. Prior booking ris equired.*

Beyond the cave, make your own zig-zagging path down the back of the ridge to the wall below. Head left on a path beside the wall, bending around the base of **Wheeldon Hill**. Turn left onto a lane and descend for about 300 metres to a rough tarmac track on the right.

**7.** Follow this, gently descending to a sharp bend by a junction of footpaths. Leave the track and go straight ahead over a stile

onto a bridleway along a grassy lane. This undulates over the headwaters of the **River Dove** — crossing the **Beggars Bridge** and then some marshy ground on **stepping stones**. A wall line now leads to a **barn** beside a gate.

**8.** Go through the gate, bend left around the rear of the barn, and take the track diagonally up the valley side. Leave this onto a lane end to head left into **Longnor**. Turn right and descend on this road back to the start to complete the walk. ♦

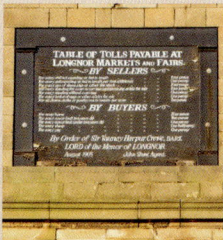

### Longnor Market

*Standing proud above the Craft Centre and Coffee Shop – once a grand Market Hall – and the cobbled square below, is a stone plaque listing buyers and sellers market fees from its heyday in the late 1800s. But when the railways came to Derbyshire and Shropshire, they avoided the steep sided Dove and Manifold valleys. Sidelined by these new transport links, Longnor's market sadly soon declined and perished.*

*Hen Cloud squats on the horizon beyond the Roaches*

# Hen Cloud

*A walk on the Peak District's wild side with secretive valleys and a couple of fabulous viewpoints*

**What to expect:**
*Secret valleys, gritstone edges, steep slopes, rough moorland paths, some boggy sections.*

**Distance/Time:** 7 kilometres/ 4½ miles. Allow 3 hours

**Start:** Layby directly below Hen Cloud opposite Windygates Farm (several other laybys also available along the road)

**Grid Ref:** SK 006 616

**Ordnance Survey Map:** Explorer OL24 Peak District: White Peak area: *Buxton, Bakewell, Matlock & Dovedale*

**After the Walk:** The Roaches Tea Rooms, Paddock Farm, Upper Holme ST13 8TY | 01538 300345 | www.roachestearooms.co.uk

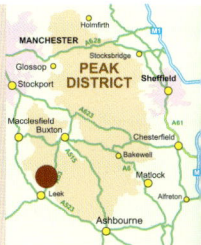

### Walk Outline

*A stroll down a lane leads to a pretty ford in Upper Hulme, before a concessionary footpath rises to Dains Mill. Head up the secretive Churnet Valley onto the Staffordshire Moorlands at Ramshaw Rocks, whose edge is a little more challenging than its Derbyshire cousins, but offers good views from the summit. A wilder series of paths then lead out past moorland farms to Hen Cloud, followed by a steep but easy ascent to fabulous views. The return takes the easiest way down.*

### Hen Cloud

Hen Cloud is a prominent gritstone outcrop rising sharply above Upper Hulme and the Meerbrook valley. It is part of the same escarpment edge as the Roaches to the north but is separated from them by a fault line which has made a dry valley. There are fabulous 360 degree views over Tittlesworth Reservoir, the Roaches and Ramshaw Rocks. On clear days the views are exceptional, stretching over 80 miles. Look out for distant peaks including Snowdon and the Carneddau, the Wrekin, Long Mynd, Plynlimon and Cadair Berwyn.

'Winking Man' rocks

Peregrine

## The Walk

**1.** Head down the country lane to **Upper Hulme**, and continue through a collection of small-scale industrial works to the pretty river **bridge and ford**. Immediately after the ford, turn left onto a concrete track, a concessionary path leading to 'Dains Mill'.

*This former corn and flour mill dates from the early 1600s, but fell into disuse in the 1940s after storm damage to one of the ponds. It was a complete ruin by 2004, when extensive restoration work began.*

**2.** Cross the **stream** by the former mill. Immediately after a gate, fork right onto a grassy path beside a wooden fence, which then roughly follows the stream. **Wooden boardwalks** lead to a boggy path in the bottom of a narrow **wooded valley**, which widens suddenly at a gate into a grassy valley. The path now rises to the left of a **ruined building**.

**3.** Turn right along a wall line and cross the stream. Ascend a grassy track, then turn right on another grassy track to **Naychuch Farm**. Follow yellow-topped concessionary path waymarkers around/across grassy fields to avoid the farmyard. Rejoining the farm driveway, head right towards the main road.

**4.** Immediately before the road, fork left onto a footpath. Rise up through gorse and heather towards the spiky-topped **Ramshaw Rocks**. At a country lane, follow this leftwards and around a sharp corner. Then take a footpath rightwards between old **stone gateposts**.

**5.** As the path rises up the rocky ridgeline, it initially skirts some distance left of the edge, before

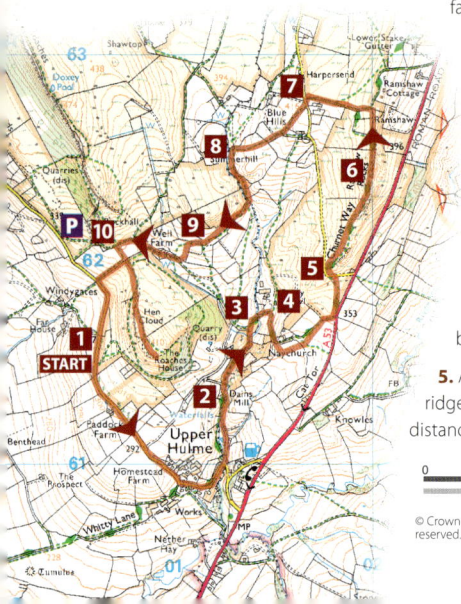

0 _____ 1 km
_____ ½ mile

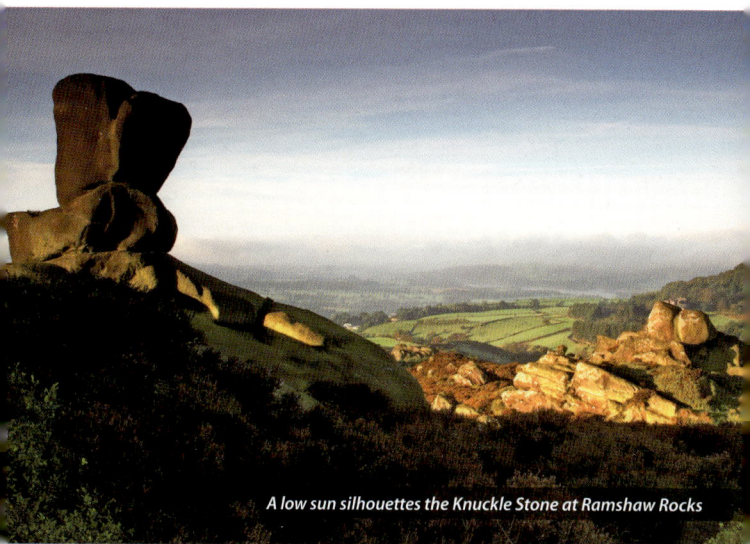

*A low sun silhouettes the Knuckle Stone at Ramshaw Rocks*

moving closer to the ridgeline as the way steepens to the **summit rocks**. It's also worth taking one or two of the many rougher paths towards some of the interestingly shaped rocks along the edge before the summit.

**6.** About 50 metres beyond the summit the path veers left off the edge then along to a **drystone wall**. Cross the next field, then follow the wall line around a corner to the left and down a rutted **bridleway** to **Blue Hills Farm**, passing just right of the **farm buildings** and out to the road.

**7.** Cross the road and take a footpath by **Misty Hill**'s driveway. Cross rough heather then keep a wall to your left. Ignore the first gate stile to your left, instead going through the second one to cross a paddock. Then follow a vague path across rough grass, bending gently right as if towards **Summerhill farmhouse** across the valley to your right.

**8.** Towards the base of this field, bend left to contour just above a stream line for around 300 metres. Cross the **stream** at a walkers' gate-stile; **stepping stones** ease the way at first, then you'll need to find

*Hen Cloud's steep scarp side gives great views towards the Roaches*

the more solid tussocks as you rise up the far bank. Go through a gate into a field, rise uphill briefly, then cross back over the wall at a stile. Contour below the **small rounded hill** to the right, aiming towards Hen Cloud.

*In early summer, look out for the antics of juvenile peregrines learning the art of flying and hunting from their parents.*

*Peregrines are one of the fastest creatures on the planet, reaching speeds of 200mph when stooping to catch their prey. They feed on smaller birds such as pigeons and collared doves, which they catch in mid-air.*

**9.** Leave this field through a farmer's gate by a pair of sycamore trees, then cross straight to a metal gate. Follow the lefthand wall down to cross the **farmyard** drive just left of a **blue barn**. Bend right in the field below the barn following a fingerpost towards 'The Roaches'. Cross the **stream** where you can, heading left of **farm buildings** and exit the far end of the field across a tiny corner of access land to a grassy sheep pasture. Cross diagonally over this, turn left immediately beyond the wall line, then cross straight back over the pasture at the next walkers' gate.

**10.** A clear path now leads directly up onto the **ridge of Hen Cloud**. Enjoy the

360 degree view from the top then, to avoid difficult ground, retrace your steps back to the grassy pasture. Turn left as you enter the grassy pasture and follow the wall line down to the road. Turn left to return to the second layby down the road where you started to complete the walk. ♦

### Antarctic explorers and wallabies

*Hen Cloud was once part of Swythamley Manor, owned for 150 years by the globe-trotting Brocklehurst family (Macclesfield silk pioneers). The second Baronet Brocklehurst, Philip Lee, was the assistant geologist on Shackleton's 1907-1909 Nimrod Expedition to Antarctica. It was from his brother Courtney's zoo at Roaches Hall, that wallabies were released into the wild in the 1930s. Keep an eye out for them – rare sightings still occur today.*

*The path to Back Tor at sunset*

# Lose Hill

*Was this once Wessex's hill in a battle against Northumbria of the 7th century? They had good views if so!*

**What to expect:**
*Steep slopes, country lanes, ridgeline path, short but steep rocky holloway.*

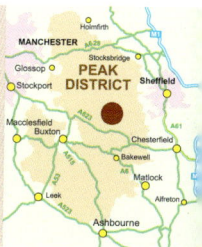

**Distance/Time:** 9 kilometres/ 6 miles. Allow 3½ hours

**Start:** Village car park, Hope

**Grid Ref:** SK 171 835

**Ordnance Survey Map:** Explorer OL1 The Peak District: Dark Peak area: *Kinder Scout, Bleaklow, Black Hill & Ladybower Reservoir*

**After the Walk:** Café Adventure, Edale Road, Hope, S33 6ZF | 01433 623313 | www.facebook.com/CafeAdventure

## Walk Outline

*A hidden footpath leads out past a mix of small fields and residential housing to larger pastures. It's roughly a straight but steep line up to Losehill's Crimea Farm. The now broader path curves up to the summit, where there's a fantastic 360 degree panorama plus a view along the ridge to Backtor Nook. The descent to Hollowford Lane is rougher underfoot, but makes a quick descent into Castleton. And finally there's a lovely path beside a stream, through fields, back to Hope.*

Lose Hill toposcope

## The Great Ridge

Lose Hill is at the easternmost end of The Great Ridge between Edale and the Hope Valley. Along with its neighbour Win Hill, Lose Hill is said to be the site of a long-forgotten battle between Saxon Wessex and Angle Northumbria. The Wessex army, camped on Lose Hill, was significantly larger, and when they sensed victory they pushed forward into the valley between the two hills. Only to be massacred by boulders rolled from Win Hill by the wily Northumbrians. How true is the tale? No-one knows, but it makes a great story and exists in written form back to the 1800s.

Meadow pipit

## The Walk

**1.** Opposite the **village car park**, take a footpath just right of the **Grasshopper Café**. This leads up steps, past a small meadow and through a snicket to a residential road. Follow this to a T-junction and cross the larger road.

**2.** From here it's roughly 1.5 kilometres towards **Lose Hill**: virtually straight ahead all the way to a **prominent barn** on the hillside. On the way, you'll pass through a succession of paths through small fields, cross a sagging **suspension bridge** over a little-used **railway line** and pass a small **stables** soon after the bridge. There's also a paralleling short track at one point; the footpath keeps to the right. As you get further from the village, the fields get larger, and the hill steeper.

**3.** Cross a small **boardwalk bridge** shortly below the **barn**. Shortly above the barn, the path takes a left across the hillside and above a **house**, before veering right and uphill again. As the final summit approaches, fork right and over a couple of stiles to enter **access land**, then rise up a steep **stone pitched path** to **Lose Hill summit**.

*There are fantastic 360 degree views from the top. From right to left there's a great view of Win Hill, Ladybower Reservoir and*

The distinctive sculptural rock cairn at Back Tor Nook

*Derwent Edge, out across the Noe (Edale) Valley to the Kinder plateau and along the 'Great Ridge' to Back Tor, Hollins Cross and Mam Tor. The view down into the Hope Valley isn't bad either.*

**4.** Enjoy the panorama at the summit, then head left along the **ridgeline** towards Mam Tor, leaving access land at a stile. At the top of **Back Tor** an impressive **cairn** marks the start of a short but steep descent on the ridge.

**5.** Cross the wall by a stile, then immediately fork left twice in quick succession to head diagonally down a long grassy path (concessionary bridleway). It may be boggy just before you pass a couple of small stands of **woodland**, then bend right above a wall line. The path braids a little here; if you head high to avoid a muddy section you'll likely have a steeper rocky descent down to the wall line.

**6.** Turn left at a **five-ways crossing of paths** and down an often damp **rocky holloway**. Emerge onto the top of a lane, descend this to a junction, then turn right

Lose Hill, Back Tor and Hollins Cross on the Great Ridge

and continue the descent to a T-junction with the main road in **Castleton**.

**7.** Turn left and pass **The Peak Hotel**. Near a bend left in the road, take a stony lane (public footpath) rightwards towards Hope. This ends at a **stream**; turn right here and go through a gate into sheep pasture. There's now a lovely waterside path for about 500 metres to a sharp bend left in the stream. Veer right here to a stile in the far right corner of the field.

**8.** You now cross several small grassy fields, then take care across an unexpected **railway line** — a continuation of the one you crossed earlier on the suspension bridge. Despite appearances this is still in use: it leads to the Hope Cement Works. Cross another field, then follow a wire fence line marking the field boundary with the **stream valley** back to a country lane, with one brief, but obvious, shortcut across a longer loop of stream.

**9.** Turn left down the lane, passing a **pinfold** just before you re-enter **Hope**.

*The rules on the pinfold here date from 1947 but pinfolds were a common method of dealing with stray animals in Medieval times. Often a stick was carved with a notch to*

represent each animal. After being split, one half went to the landowner, and the other to the 'pinder', or pinfold-keeper. Once the strays' owner had paid the landowner, he was given their half-stick. This was taken to the pinder and 'tallied', or matched, with the other half and the animals released.

Turn left onto the main **village road** to complete the walk. ♦

### 'Ward's Piece'

The other accepted name for the summit of Lose Hill — Ward's Piece — comes from the purchase of the summit area by the Sheffield and District Federation of the Ramblers in 1945. They dedicated it to their founder (a dedicated, lifelong advocate of rambling) GHB Ward before handing it over to the National Trust to preserve for everyone to enjoy. This was one of the earliest forms of access land.

*Shutlingsloe is sometimes called the 'Cheshire Matterhorn'*

# Shutlingsloe

*Head up through Macclesfield Forest on the easy route to the summit of the 'Cheshire Matterhorn'*

**What to expect:**
*Forestry tracks, and lane; stone-flagged moorland path, steep final ascent*

**Distance/Time:** 7.5 kilometres/ 5 miles. Allow 3-3½ hours

**Start:** Trentabank Ranger Office Car Park, Macclesfield Forest

**Grid Ref:** SJ 961 711

**Ordnance Survey Map:** Explorer OL24 Peak District: White Peak area: *Buxton, Bakewell, Matlock & Dovedale*

**After the Walk:** The Leathers Smithy, Clarke Lane, Sutton, Macclesfield SK11 0NE | 01260 252 313

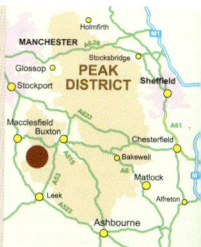

## Walk Outline

*A steep rise through Macclesfield Forest leads to open moorland on Piggford Moor. Stone flags ease the way over boggy terrain followed by a short but steep ascent to the summit. Return the same way to the edge of the forestry, continuing on forestry trails to the Standing Stone car park. A narrower forestry path roughly parallels the road, then crosses the road to gain a path beside the Bollin Brook. Finally, it's just a short stroll to a viewpoint over the heronry at Trentabank.*

'The only way is up'

## Shutlingsloe

Shutlingsloe stands proud of the surrounding countryside like a triangular beacon, which gives rise to its local name of the 'Cheshire Matterhorn'. At 506 metres high, it is second only to Shining Tor as the highest peak in Cheshire. While its prominent pyramidal shape is most striking from the Wildboarclough side, this walk opts for the gentler approach from Macclesfield Forest. You'll be well rewarded by views from the summit, which are particularly impressive; and the grassy top is a great place to sit and watch the world go by.

Golden plover

*Wide views from Shutlingsloe's summit*

## The Walk

**1.** Leaving the **car park** with **Trentabank Reservoir** on your left, follow multicoloured banded waymarkers on a track parallel to the road. Go through 'A bars' and bear right, following red, blue-black and yellow bands. Continue straight ahead where the **Gritstone Trail** forks right — more steeply uphill now. Join a **forestry road** and head left. Within 100 metres reach a path junction by a gate across the track, and turn right.

*Although the pine plantation of Macclesfield Forest matches today's*

*convention of forestry being an area of woodland, the original Macclesfield Forest had nothing to do with trees. Rather it was a royal hunting reserve where the King's permission was required to hunt wild boar and deer.*

**2.** You're now following red and blue-black banded waymarkers up a wide **forestry trail** that is steep in places. A squeeze stile by a large wooden gate marks the current upper limit of the forest; undoubtedly, the upper section of forestry will be replanted in the lifetime of this book. Bend left on a wide track to

rise gently above the **forestry line**, then fork right, following signs to 'Shutlingsloe' at both junctions.

**3.** Join the **'Langley to Wildboarclough'** **footpath** at the entrance to access land. You now follow a **stone flagged path** across open moorland, which eases the going over intermittently boggy ground to the **base of Shutlingsloe**.

**4.** Go through a gate stile and turn right on a **stone flagged path** across **Piggford Moor**, (leaving the Wildboarclough footpath), now heading direct to the base of Shutlingsloe's pyramid top. A high **step stile** with gate at the start of the final short but steep ascent leads up some surprisingly tall **stone steps**. Bend right, then up more gently to the **trig point at the summit**.

*Piggford Moor is thought to be the southernmost breeding range of the golden plover. A relative of the lapwing, this bird is rare in the UK. It is thought there are somewhere between 1 and 24 breeding pairs on Piggford Moor. The moor is also home to other rare species such as short-eared owl and merlin.*

*Looking down from Shutlingsloe over the Clough Brook valley*

**5.** Now retrace your steps back down to the 'Wildboarclough to Langley' footpath and return on your outward path to the edge of access land at the top of **Macclesfield Forest**. Follow the path down to a bench and rejoin the forest trail from earlier.

**6.** Turn right along this, away from your outward route, towards 'Standing Stone'. Either continue along the forest trail down through **Ferriser Farm** then back uphill, or take a pleasant if slightly muddy shortcut on a narrow footpath that continues ahead at a sharp bend left, leading past a 'Walkers only' sign. This rises beside a wall line then gently descends to rejoin the forest track.

**7.** Immediately before the road by the **Standing Stone Car Park**, take a narrower rougher path left towards Trentabank, paralleling the road. This leads downhill through the forest. Cross the road, the path now descends to a gate, then bears right signed towards 'Trentabank'. Pass a **pond**, then turn left, still following Trentabank signs (and now occasional black/blue banded waymarker posts). This descends near the **Bollin Brook**, then bends left to return to the road.

**8.** Crossing the road again, the ongoing path roughly follows the line of the road through woodland on the far side. At a

set of 'A bars', follow the green banded route through them to rejoin the quiet road, heading left. Just beyond a layby, the path re-enters woodland to the right. This takes a short loop to a viewpoint over the **Trentabank heronry,** then bends back to the **Ranger Centre car park** to complete the walk. ♦

### Noisy heronry

*The heronry at Trentabank is thought to be the largest in the Peak District, with more than 20 pairs of birds breeding each year between March and June. They nest in the secluded larch plantation at the eastern end of the forestry. In winter, goldeneye, goosander and siskin are frequent visitors, and red deer can be heard bellowing across the reservoir in the rutting season in October.*

*Thorpe Cloud is a solitary limestone summit known as a 'reef knoll'*

# Thorpe Cloud

*High above the iconic River Dove, this viewpoint gives stunning views across the southern tip of the Pennines*

**What to expect:**
*Pasture, steep slopes, stepping stones, riverside path and green lanes .*

**Distance/Time:** 6.5 kilometres/ 4 miles. Allow 2½-3 hours

**Start:** Narlows Lane car park, Thorpe

**Grid Ref:** SK 163 504

**Ordnance Survey Map:** Explorer OL24  Peak District: White Peak area: *Buxton, Bakewell, Matlock & Dovedale*

**After the Walk:** The Old Dog, Spend Lane, Thorpe, Ashbourne DE6 2AT | 01335 350 990 | www.theolddog.co.uk

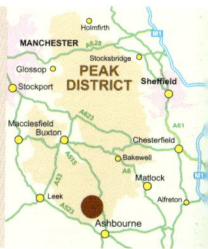

## Walk Outline

*The route descends from the upper part of Thorpe village into Thorpe Pastures and past the rifle range. All routes up Thorpe Cloud are steep, but the climb from this direction is the shortest. There's an optional short ridge scramble over the true summit for the adventurous, then onto the more popular summit, which has a fantastic view over Dovedale. A steep descent leads to the famous stepping stones and along the River Dove to Coldwall Bridge, then up an ancient track back to the village.*

## Thorpe Cloud

Where else in the Peak District can you find a hill with a great viewpoint over such a well-known honeypot as Dovedale? Add in a very brief but enjoyable — but entirely optional — narrow rocky ridgeline and a series of stepping stones below and you'll be hard pressed to find a better short but energetic walk in the region. The name Cloud derives from the Middle English 'clud' or 'clod' — meaning a mass of hill or rock. So, presumably our ancestors thought clouds looked like rocks?

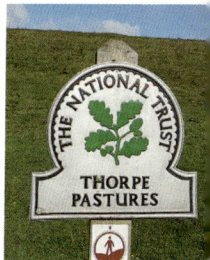
*'For everyone, for ever'*

*Rockrose*

## The Walk

**1.** From the car park, cross the junction by the **Old Dog pub** and head downhill past the **petrol station** to a sharp bend left by the **Peveril of the Peak Hotel** and fork right onto a footpath.

**2.** Cross two small grassy fields then enter **Thorpe Pastures** (National Trust land). Head left beside the wall — if red flags are flying (rifle range in use), keep to the perimeter of the field — then bear right, directly towards Thorpe Cloud, as the field widens to the left. Head right of a **barn** to a gate.

**3.** Rise up the steep flanks of **Thorpe Cloud**; as the gradient steepens and becomes rockier towards the summit, bear left on a grassier line bypassing the **true summit**. (The adventurous can zigzag up scrambly rock to a lovely short and rocky narrow ridgeline). Head along the continuing grassy ridgeline to the **viewpoint over the Dove Valley**.

**4.** Enjoy the view then take a well-worn steep descent to the right of the ridgeline. *At the bottom, the exposed limestone can be slippery and awkward.*

**5.** Cross the river via **stepping stones** and head downstream along the track to a **footbridge**. (Note: If the stepping stones are flooded, the narrow footpath on the nearer bank may still be passable down to the bridge).

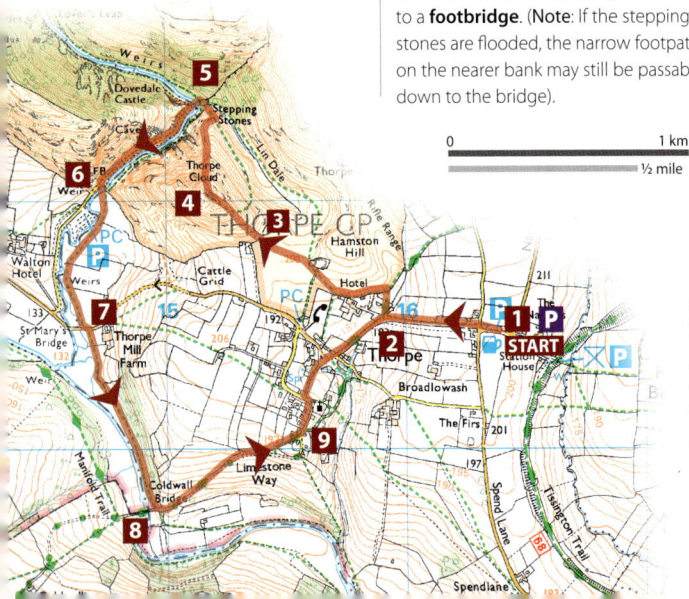

Dovedale's river crossing is an ever-popular 'mini-adventure'

**6.** Cross the footbridge then turn right into fields. The footpath follows the river downstream through grassy pastures to a **road bridge**.

**7.** Cross over the road and continue near the river for roughly 700 metres to a **further bridge** (carrying a former road).

**8.** Turn left onto a vehicle track and rise out of the valley. At a fingerpost, turn left into an upper field corner, leading to a narrow **green lane** between houses.

**9.** Turn left onto tarmac and down past the **church**. Turn right at the junction by the **village hall** and down to the main road. Turn right along pavement back to the **hotel** where you rejoin your outward route and head back uphill to the start to complete the walk. ♦

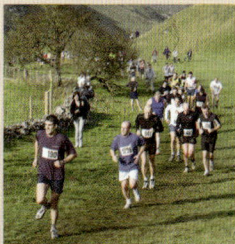

### Doing the 'Dovedale Dash'

*On the first Sunday in November, about 1,500 runners of all shapes and sizes gather on the fields at Thorpe Pasture for the 'Dovedale Dash'. Just under 5 miles in length, this local race shares some of the riverside paths used by this walk. Many runners will choose to forgo the stepping stones, instead 'dashing' through the river. From autumn until late spring, boggy sections are likely along riverside paths.*

*Alderman's Hill seen across Dovestone Reservoir*

# Alderman's Hill

*A lesser-known viewpoint with fabulous views over the Dovestone Reservoirs, Saddleworth Moor and Harrop valley*

**What to expect:**
*Rough hollow way, country lane, access tracks, open moorland, grassy descent.*

**Distance/Time:** 5 kilometres/ 3 miles. Allow 2-3 hours

**Start:** Roadside parking outside Pobgreen Church

**Grid Ref:** SE 007063

**Ordnance Survey Map:** Explorer OL1 The Peak District: Dark Peak area: *Kinder Scout, Bleaklow, Black Hill & Ladybower Reservoir*

**After the Walk:** Church Inn, Church lane, Uppermill, Oldham OL3 6LW | 01457 820 902 | www.churchinnsaddleworth.co.uk

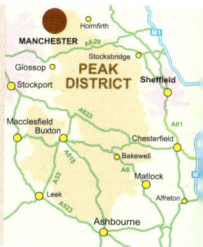

## Walk Outline

*A rough path leads past a farmyard to a steep and sustained grassy ascent onto the ridgeline at Slades Brow. The gradient then fades away to a pleasant undulation along the edge, then across a wide moorland plateau to Alderman's Brow, with its fabulous viewpoint over the Dovestone, Yeoman Hey and Greenfield Reservoirs. A path along the plateau edge leads to the Obelisk — with a bonus view over Uppermill and Harrop Dale. Finally, a diagonal path returns across boggy ground via country lanes down to the church.*

## Alderman's Hill

According to folklore, Alder and Alphin were two giants who lived on Alderman's Hill and Alphin Hill. They both fell in love with a beautiful nymph, Rimmon, who lived in the Chew Brook between the hills. Fighting over her, they hurled rocks until Alphin was killed. But Rimmon loved Alphin, not Alder. And when Alphin died, she threw herself off a crag. Leaving Alder alone on his hill. Like many such tales, was this a retelling of some old battle between rival armies? No-one knows, but the legend persists.

*Rocks on Alderman's Hill*

*Cotton grass*

## The Walk

**1.** Facing the **church**, take a footpath immediately right of the church wall, being careful to locate the correct path, which heads straight rather than diagonally uphill. Bear slightly right after a gate and head all the way up a driveway to **Ivy Bank Farm**, to reach a narrow country lane.

**2.** A footpath immediately opposite continues steeply up a **shallow, dry valley** to the top of a field, exiting onto a green lane. This goes more gently uphill to a gate at the entrance to **access land**, where the righthand wall fades briefly. Stay just right of the dry valley for the easiest line to a footpath waymarker at a nick in the ridge ahead.

**3.** Head right on a faint path. This initially aims towards a wooden stile, then bends right to take a line between a tumbledown drystone wall and wire fence. The views now open out significantly to your right over Pobgreen and Harrop Vale, with an impressive collection of drystone walls below marking out a rectangular field system.

*Cotton grass is a type of bog-loving sedge whose white shimmering downy flowers resemble that of cotton. Its fibres are too brittle to form thread, but they have been used in the past as a*

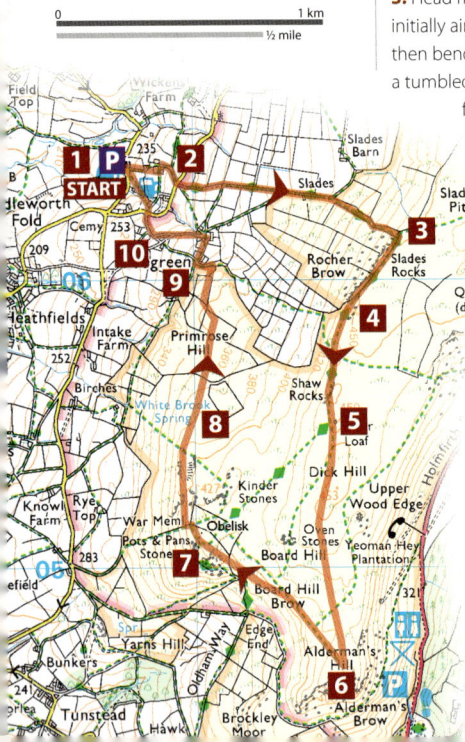

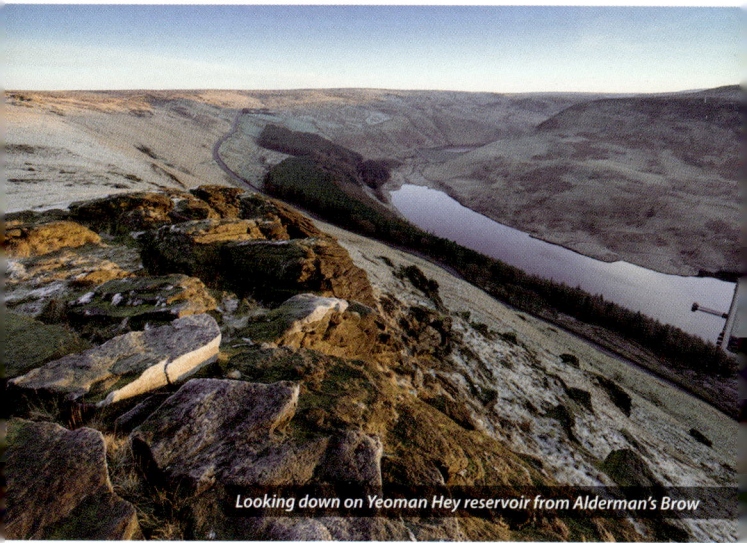

*Looking down on Yeoman Hey reservoir from Alderman's Brow*

*cheaper alternative to down for pillows, and made into paper and candle wicks, too.*

**4.** The path stays with the wire fence as the wall line veers right, then crosses a slightly awkward 'pallet stile' when the wire fence takes a corner rightwards then divides by an **outcrop of rounded sideways-slanting boulders**. Take the leftmost of two more prominent paths, heading towards a prominent **group of three small boulders**.

**5.** Cross a **stony track** just left of a gas pipeline marker (a faded orange marker).

The wide grassy track now heads out across **open moorland**, dipping gently to a slight saddle (where a narrower path joins from the left) then rising again to the **viewpoint of Alderman's Brow**.

**6.** Turning around, you now take a grassy track left of the one you arrived on (the middle of three grassy paths running just inland of a plateau edge). This takes an arcing route to the **obelisk, or war memorial, at 'Pots and Pans'** on the far edge of the plateau, dipping over some incipient valley heads on the way. (**Note:** If you drop significantly off the

*Looking south across Dovestones Reservoir and up the Chew Valley*

plateau edge you've probably taken a path too far to the left!).

**7.** Cross a stile over a wire fence then some rusty **iron railings** lead beside the **memorial**. After visiting the memorial, turn right at the end of the railings. Follow a broken wall rising very gently uphill and through a gap near its end. The path now heads diagonally downhill passing above an **old quarry** on your left.

**8.** As a dry stone wall comes close from the right, the path aims across boggier ground for a prominent **pair of gatepost stones** about 400 metres distant. Bend

left at these and down to a semi-ruined wall. Stay uphill of the wall and a **small grassy mound**, then turn left with the wall as it makes a corner near a wire fence. Head down to a stile to leave access land.

**9.** Pass left of a **white house** then turn right to pass immediately in front of the house. Take a gravel driveway which bends left at a farm and down to a road junction. Turn left and descend to the **Cross Keys pub**, bending sharp right on the way.

**10.** Cross the road and descend steps

into the pub car park. Turn left; the continuing footpath is hard to find, but is at the back of the car park and to the left of outside seating.

Descend this path back to the car park by the church, to complete the walk. ♦

### Focus or folly?

*The war memorial at Pots and Pans has a commanding view over the Saddleworth valley. The obelisk's location was chosen so that it could be seen from all five villages in the Saddleworth community. It cost an estimated £2,000 in 1919 and some people said the money would have been better spent on improving local medical facilities. Nonetheless, the monument still attracts a sizeable crowd for the annual Remembrance Sunday walk from the church below.*

*The 'hidden viewpoint' is located between the Litton and Cressbrook tunnels*

# Monsal Hidden View

*A lovely secret, hidden viewpoint over the River Wye is now accessible after the reopening of the Monsal tunnels*

**Distance/Time:** 8.5 kilometres/ 5½ miles. Allow 3½-4 hours

**Start:** Tideswell Dale car park

**Grid Ref:** SK 154 741

**Ordnance Survey Map:** Explorer OL24 Peak District: White Peak area: *Buxton, Bakewell, Matlock & Dovedale*

**After the Walk:** High Nellys Café, 2 Bank Square, Tideswell, Buxton SK17 8LA | 07906 160 691

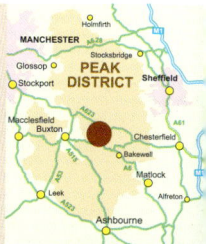

## Walk Outline

*Starting from the Tideswell Dale car park, descend beside the brook into Litton. Climb onto the Monsal Trail and head through the tunnels on this former rail line. The secret view overlooks the river bend near Cressbrook. At the end of the Cressbrook tunnel, head down past Cressbrook Mill. A country lane eases part of the ascent up Cressbrook Dale, then rough woodland, open fields and lanes lead back to Litton Dale. A roadside footpath completes the circuit back to the car park.*

## Monsal's Hidden View

The River Wye is one of the best known of the Peak District rivers, home to a thriving population of brown and rainbow trout, and a major tributary of the Derwent. The Monsal Trail runs above its banks along the former Monsal railway line. After closure of the line in 1968, the tunnels were sealed for safety reasons. Sandwiched between the Cressbrook and Litton tunnels, this grand viewpoint perched high above an impressive bend on the limestone gorge of the River Wye was lost until the re-opening of the tunnels in 2011 as a multi-use cycle and walking route.

*Monsal Trail signpost*

*Wild garlic, or 'ramsons'*

## The Walk

**1.** Exit **Tideswell Dale car park** from its far end and head along a **tarmac trail** beside a brook. This crosses over the brook a couple of times, and passes below a small **cave** and high **limestone crags** just before a country lane.

**2.** Take this leftwards and into **Litton**. Look for a sewage **pumping station** to your right opposite the second group of houses. Immediately beyond this, take a fairly well-hidden footpath to the right. This leads past **Riverside House** and across the river on a narrow **footbridge**.

**3.** Rise up steps over the **mill race**; the path then zigzags up the steep hillside to reach the **Monsal Trail**. Turn left along this; it's now easy going along the Trail for the next 350 metres to the **Litton Tunnel**. As you exit the 470 metres tunnel, the track continues on a short perched balcony with the **Hidden View** to your left.

**4.** Having admired the view, continue through the 430 metre long **Cressbrook Tunnel**. As the tunnel cutting ends, turn sharp left off the Monsal Trail. Contour along the hillside (ignore a fainter narrow rising path forking left), and under some power lines, then descend steeply on a hairpin set of rocky **limestone steps** to a **footbridge**.

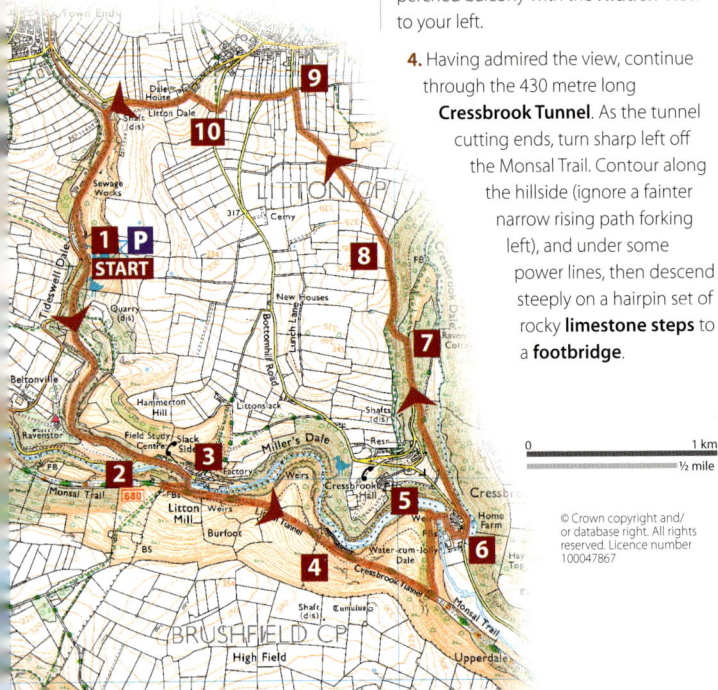

Limestone crags at Water cum Jolly seen from the ravine by the mill

*Along the river, watch out for the occasional white flash of a small, fast-flying bird moving from rock to rock along the river. Only when they're stationary, does it become much clearer that these small birds are dippers. Their name comes from their characteristic dipping bob as they perch on rocks, searching for insect larvae in the water below.*

**5.** Cross the river, enjoy the views of Water cum Jolly, then take a path rightwards towards the **restored mill** (now private apartments), bending several times in front of the mill to reach a lane.

**6.** Turn left onto this (towards Litton) and stay on this to rise gently to a hairpin bend some 800 metres distant. Pass a side turn to the right shortly before the hairpin, then at the **hairpin bend** continue ahead on a wide track through deciduous woodland.

*In early summer the pervasive smell of wild garlic and a tumbling swathe of white flowers flows down the bank to the right. The leaves and flowers are edible and are said to lower cholesterol and act as a mild disinfectant. But beware; before flowering it can be easily confused with the poisonous but far rarer Lily of the Valley.*

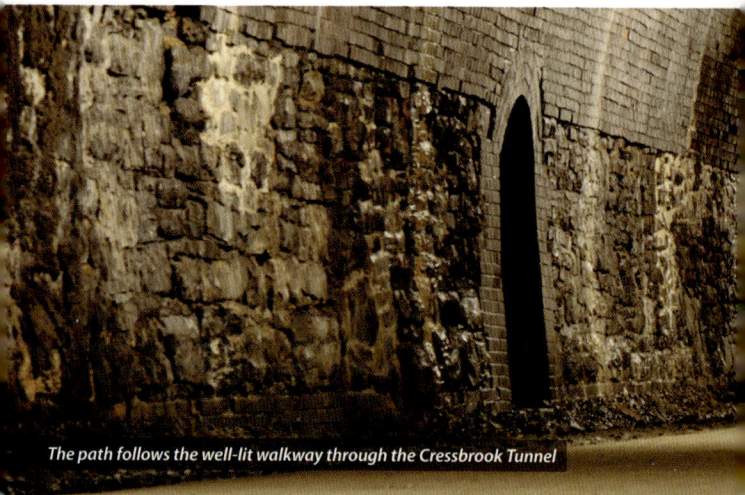

*The path follows the well-lit walkway through the Cressbrook Tunnel*

**7.** Fork left at the edge of woodland onto a narrower path to remain in the trees. Bend left as it threatens to leave the woodland once more, rising steeply with steps on the very steepest section. Towards the top of the woodland, merge rightwards with a gently rising path. This can be narrow or overgrown in summer in places beside a wall at plateau level.

**8.** After about 500 metres go through a narrow gate in the wall and veer diagonally across four grassy fields in a roughly straight line. Cross a **green lane** then continue down through two more fields into a **shallow valley** bending gently leftwards. Rise directly uphill in the next, and final, field to a country lane.

**9.** Turn left onto a **farm track**, then immediately left onto the **lane** on a bend. Pass a **barn** on your left then take a footpath straight ahead through a narrow **squeeze stile** where the road bends left. Stay beside the wall to your right across three short fields, then bear diagonally across the next stone walled field beside a wire fence — which then funnels you across the base of the next field to a road.

**10.** Cross this lane, descending diagonally right across the next field. A short path now heads left around a

building to reach a country lane. Take its pavement leftwards, heading downhill to a junction with a larger road on the edge of **Tideswell**. Cross this to keep the pavement, head downhill back towards the **car park**, crossing back just after the sewage works to gain an off-road footpath which takes you directly back to the car park to complete the walk. ♦

### Dark, satanic mills?

*Nowadays, these modern, refurbished mill apartments look very desirable, with their grand facades emphasising their Industrial Revolution heritage. Cressbrook Mill was established by Richard Arkwright and Litton Mill by locals Ellis Needham and Thomas Firth. However, in the mid-1800s they offered abysmal conditions to workhouse orphans. To modern minds, the mills' indentured child labour was effectively a form of slavery.*

*Dawn 'catchlight' on Over Owler Tor*

# Burbage Valley Tors

*Burbage Brook and a series of tors with fabulous views over Carl Wark and the Burbage Valley*

**What to expect:**
*Well worn paths, moorland tracks, short holloway and edge ascent and descent*

**Distance/Time:** 8.5 kilometres/ 5½ miles. Allow 3-3½ hours

**Start:** Surprise View car park, near Hathersage

**Grid Ref:** SK 251 800

**Ordnance Survey Map:** Explorer OL1 The Peak District: Dark Peak area: *Kinder Scout, Bleaklow, Black Hill & Ladybower Reservoir*

**After the Walk:** Fox House pub, Hathersage Road, Longshaw, Sheffield S11 7TY | 01433 630 374

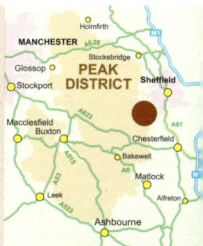

## Walk Outline

*A hollow way through the heather drops past Owler Tor to pretty Burbage Brook. Head gently upstream to Upper Burbage Bridge, where an undulating path leads to craggy edged Higger Tor — with a great viewpoint over Carl Wark and the Burbage Valley. Then drop off the back of Higger Tor across open moorland to the crags of Over Owler Tor, with its panoramic views over the Burbage Valley and Millstone Edge.*

## Over Owler Tor

There are viewpoints aplenty on this walk, with the two tors of Higger and Over Owler offering differing but equally photogenic options. Slightly elevated from the plateau, these rocky outcrops give outstanding panoramic moorland vistas over the Burbage Valley, the ancient hill fort of Carl Wark, and the unexpected cube-shaped small outcrop of Mother Cap. To the west of Higger and Over Owler there are some fantastic views across the short moorland plateau to Millstone Edge and over the Hope Valley. Below Millstone Edge is the village of Hathersage — the inspiration for Charlotte Bronte's *Jane Eyre.*

*Burbage Brook*

*Red grouse*

## The Walk

**1.** Cross the road, then take a cut-through onto access land at **Lawrence Field**, about 50 metres to the right of the bus stop. The path parallels the road, keeping to the left of the rocky outcrop of **Owler Tor**, to reach a second road access point. Take a path leading directly away from the access point, down a heathery hollow way to **Burbage Brook**.

**2.** Walk left along the **river bank** (don't cross the bridge), pass a **weir** then go across the next **footbridge**. Rise up a stone pitched path and cross a side-stream twice to follow 'Longshaw short route' arrows to the right at a path junction. This path leads up through **woodland**. About 100 metres beyond a **wooden gate**, fork sharp left (almost back on yourself) and out onto the road.

**3.** Cross the road and take the **permissive bridleway** opposite. This wide track roughly contours along below rocky moorland and **Burbage Edge**, for some 2.5 kilometres/1½ miles. *Known locally as the 'Green Drive', it has great views over Carl Wark and Higger Tor.*

*During 1808-1809, the Enclosure Acts effectively privatised the Burbage valley, sealing off a variety of packhorse and walking routes. The 5th Duke of Rutland then built Longshaw as a shooting estate, and the 'Green Drive' was constructed to ease the way for his guests heading out onto the moorland. It wasn't until the 1930s, when the National Trust acquired the land, that access was restored to the wider public.*

0            1 km
                ½ mile

*The bracken-clad slopes of Higger Tor from Carl Wark*

**4.** This reaches the road at **Upper Burbage Bridge** (which is actually two bridges) by the headwaters of the **Burbage Brook**. Head left just before the gate onto the road and take a rough path paralleling the road, fording the two headwaters.

**5.** Where this path reaches the **car park**, take the rightmost of two waymarked footpaths. This undulates along **Fiddler's Elbow** to the northern end of **Higger Tor**. Enjoy a wander around the rocks and various viewpoints — including

a window view over Carl Wark (the gritstone ringed, flat-topped tor roughly 500 metres to the south), then make your way to the western, or far, end of Higger Tor.

**6.** At this far end, a path descends to the right — off the gentler side of the edge. At the base of the steep slope, fork left to curve below the western end of the rocks and onto the plateau with its numerous faint paths criss-crossing the moorland. As you near a **sheepfold**, follow a path along its right-hand edge. About half

*Looking towards Carl Wark from Higger Tor's jumbled rocks*

way along this, fork right on a wider path towards the skyline. This well-trodden path takes you to **Over Owler Tor**, crossing over a clearly-defined path at **Winyards Nick**.

*According to palaeontologists, there are numerous signs that the area around Winyards Nick was once the site of a prehistoric settlement. Experts can make out a linear field system with clearance cairns and a clearance bank hidden beneath the heather. These date from the Bronze Age, and are of varying sizes, with some of the cairns up to 11 metres across, and forming either circles or ovals on the ground.*

**7.** As you reach the blocky edge of **Over Owler Tor**, the path passes between a pair of unfinished **millstones**. Ignore a leftwards-pointing arrow carved in one of these (stay on the main path) and scrabble up the briefly rougher and blocky edge. It's worth exploring the rocky tor, but for onward progress, head rightwards towards the highest rocks, with a view to the left to the solitary blocky outcrop of **Mother Cap** in the distance. Bend round beside the rocks of **Over Owler Tor**, then stay close to the edge and right of the main exit path (it's close to the rock with water-worn 'eyeholes').

**8.** This takes you to the start of a path descending the edge rightwards across lower moorland to the fenceline of **Millstone Edge**, with some great views over the Hope Valley. Follow the fenceline left along the top of Millstone Edge, descending to a junction of paths by a gate through the fence. Bend left with the main path which now leads through heather and between two stands of birch trees back to the **car park** to complete the walk. ♦

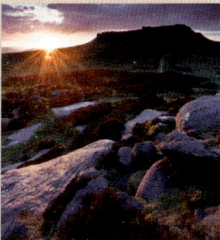

### Ritual enclosure?

*Carl Wark stands atop a gritstone tor and was previously considered to be an Iron Age fortress. However, a lack of a reliable water source within the defensible area means it would have had limited use against prolonged attack. It is now thought it may originally have been a Bronze Age ceremonial gathering location, similar to an enclosure at Gardom's Edge, which was subsequently fortified in the Dark Ages.*

*The Great Ridge extends from Mam Tor in the west to Lose Hill in the east*

# Mam Tor

*The Mother Mountain of the Peak provides a stunning view over lovely Edale and the Hope Valley*

**Distance/Time:** 8.5 kilometres/ 5½ miles. Allow 3-4 hours

**Start:** Visitor Centre car park, Castleton

**Grid Ref:** SK 149 829

**Ordnance Survey Map:** Explorer OL1 The Peak District: Dark Peak area: *Kinder Scout, Bleaklow, Black Hill & Ladybower Reservoir*

**After the Walk:** Ramblers Rest Cafe, Back Street, Millbridge, Castleton S33 8WR | 01433 620 125 | www.ramblersrest-castleton.co.uk

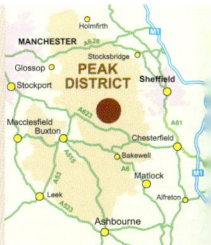

## Walk Outline

*A short walk through the back of Castleton leads to a steep grassy slope. Zigzags take the worst of the sting from this, then continuing grassy fields lead past Rowter Farm to a stony track. This leads to the Sparrowpit Road, then a grassy track leads to Mam Nick. Pitched steps take you onto the summit, and stone flags down to Hollins Cross. A sheltered holloway then leads to a gentle country lane back to Castleton.*

## Mam Tor

Mam Tor is sometimes known as the 'Shivering Mountain' due to its propensity to landslips. The paved summit area on Mam Tor hides a Bronze Age tumulus, or ritual burial site. This indicates the hill was occupied well before an Iron Age village that once dominated the summit, and whose remnants can be spotted by the expert eye.

But it's the stunning panoramic views that most people come for — looking down over Edale and Castleton, and along the lofty ridgeline to Hollins Cross.

*Above Cave Dale*

*Meadow cranesbill*

## The Walk

**1.** From the **visitor centre car park**, cross the mini roundabout and take a narrow lane between the **Three Roofs Cafe** and **ASD Blue John Jewellers**. This quickly becomes a footpath running beside a **channelled stream**. Turn right onto a road and cross a **bridge** by Carlton Emporium. Stay on the road to 'Goosehill' to the end of tarmac by 'Mayfield'. Continue ahead on a rougher surface and into permissive **open access land** at a gate. Follow a wall line on your right nearly as far as a sharp bend rightwards; then turn left.

**2.** This turn is almost back on yourself onto a faint path leading diagonally up the steep hillside. This bends sharp right and becomes wider just before a broken fence line. It's worth continuing a bit closer to the fence to see an impressive view into the steep-sided dry gorge of **Cave Dale**.

*Further down the dale is Peveril Castle — a ruined 11th century castle founded by William Peveril shortly after the Norman conquest, and which gave the new settlement of Castleton its name. In 1155 Henry II confiscated the castle and Peveril's*

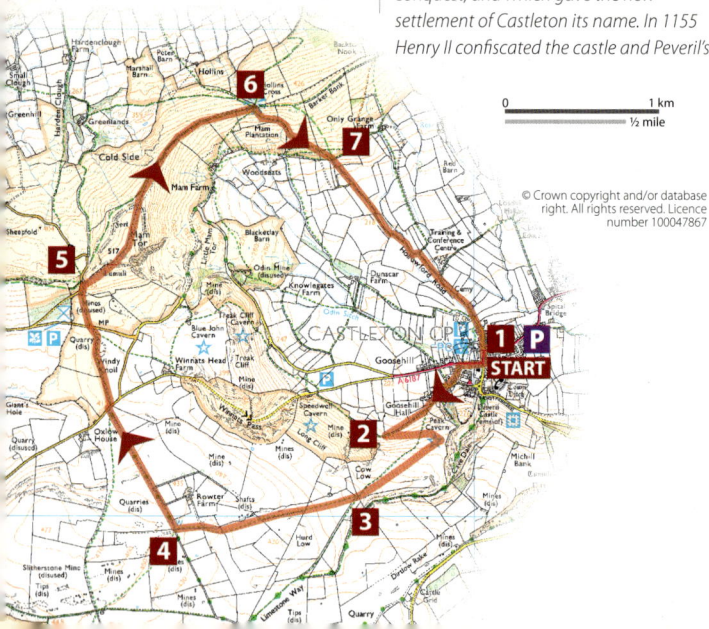

0            1 km
½ mile

Dawn's early light illuminates the Mam Tor ridge

*estates; a few years later, in 1176, he constructed the stone keep that remains today.*

**3.** After about 700 metres take a **stone step stile** across a drystone wall — leaving the permissive open access land. Pass a lone tree then ignore the grassy path ahead and fork immediately right over a broken-down wall line onto a fainter grassy path. This now maintains its rough line for 1.2 kilometres, passing one field to the left of **Rowter Farm**, and crossing several field-edge stiles on the way. There is a short and clearly waymarked section of concession path heading right of the **dewpond** (not left, as on the Ordnance Survey maps) near the farm.

*Evidence of former lead mining can be seen in numerous hollows on the hillside around here. This was a common smallholders activity in the White Peak, dating back to at least Roman times and often helped to supplement a meagre income from subsistence agriculture. However, larger mines such as the Odin were likely to have been rather more commercially organised.*

*Above the clouds at Mam Nick Pass, looking down into Edale*

**4.** Turn right onto a gravel track, which heads out to a main road. Cross slightly rightwards over this onto a vehicle track rising towards Mam Tor. Bend slightly left to cross a second road, the ongoing steep grassy track now leads more clearly to **Mam Nick**, rising up some **stone steps** towards the Mam Nick road.

**5.** Avoiding the road, now bear right through a gate onto a **paved stepped path**, which leads to the **summit trig point** with great views over Castleton and Edale. The wide **paved path** continues along the ridgeline, passing through two gates to reach **Hollins Cross** — the dip before a steep rise, with a **memorial cairn to Tom Hyatt**.

**6.** Fork right and through a gate. Two paths diverge here, take the leftmost. This **paved path** descends steeply and diagonally across the hillside, fading to a dirt track lower down. Stay on this track crossing under a **line of telegraph poles** and through a gate to reach a junction of several paths.

**7.** Go through a second gate and down a **rocky bridleway** leading to the top of **Hollowford Road**.

*Holloways are ancient trackways, whose upper surface has been worn down below the surrounding countryside over the centuries by the constant passage of people and pack animals. Many of these would*

*have been medieval routes transporting salt, corn and cloth.*

Follow this tarmac lane down into **Castleton**, turning right at a junction near a playground sign then joining the main road through Castleton on a bend. Turn right along this and through Castleton to the **Three Roofs Cafe** by the mini roundabout. The entrance to the **car park** is opposite, so completing the walk. ♦

### 'Shivering Mountain'

*Mam Tor's geology is the reason behind its so-called 'shivers' or landslips. These are caused by a weak layer of shale (a form of mudstone which splits easily along its layers and slides when waterlogged) lying between limestone and gritstone strata. The most famous of these dramatic landslips destroyed the now abandoned A625 in 1974; but similar examples can be found nearby at Mam Nick, Eyam and Hucklow Edges, too.*

# Useful Information

### Visit Peak District & Derbyshire
The Peak's official tourism website covers everything from accommodation and special events to attractions and adventure. **www.visitpeakdistrict.com**

### Peak District National Park
The Peak District National Park website also has information on things to see and do, plus a host of practical details to help you plan your visit. **www.peakdistrict.gov.uk**

### Visitor Centres
The main Visitor Centres provide free information on everything from accommodation and transport to what's on and walking advice.

| | | |
|---|---|---|
| Bakewell | 01629 816558 | bakewell@peakdistrict.gov.uk |
| Castleton | 01433 620679 | castleton@peakdistrict.gov.uk |
| Moorland Centre, Edale | 01433 670207 | edale@peakdistrict.gov.uk |
| Upper Derwent | 01433 650953 | derwentinfo@peakdistrict.gov.uk |

### Rail Travel
Several railway services cross the National Park:

Hope Valley line

Derwent Valley line

Manchester to Buxton line

Manchester to Glossop line

Manchester to Huddersfield line (Transpennine express)

Information is available from National Rail Enquiries on 03457 484 950 or **www.nationalrail.co.uk**

### Bus Travel
The Peak District's towns and many of the villages are served by bus. Information is available from Traveline on 0871 200 22 33 or **www.traveline.info**

### Weather
Online weather forecasts for the Peak District are available from the Met Office at **www.metoffice.gov.uk/public/weather/mountain-forecasts/peak-district** or the MWIS can be more specific – **www.mwis.org.uk/english-welsh-forecast/PD**